WOMEN
WITH WINGS

WOMEN PILOTS
OF WORLD WAR II

BY SHANNON BAKER MOORE

CONTENT CONSULTANT
JACQUELINE LUEDTKE, PHD
ASSOCIATE PROFESSOR OF AERONAUTICS
EMBRY-RIDDLE AERONAUTICAL UNIVERSITY

Essential Library

An Imprint of Abdo Publishing | abdopublishing.com

ABDOPUBLISHING.COM

Published by Abdo Publishing, a division of ABDO, PO Box 398166, Minneapolis, Minnesota 55439. Copyright © 2017 by Abdo Consulting Group, Inc. International copyrights reserved in all countries. No part of this book may be reproduced in any form without written permission from the publisher. Essential Library™ is a trademark and logo of Abdo Publishing.

Printed in the United States of America, North Mankato, Minnesota
112016
012017

THIS BOOK CONTAINS RECYCLED MATERIALS

Cover Photo: US National Archives and Records Administration
Interior Photos: Courtesy of The WASP Archive, Texas Woman's University, Denton, TX, 4–5, 11, 78–79, 86 (left), 86 (right), 87 (left), 87 (upper right), 87 (lower right); US Air Force, 7, 13, 37, 64–65, 88–89; Luigi Rados/Library of Congress, 16–17; Smithsonian National Air and Space Museum (NASM 81-3423), 19; Smithsonian National Air and Space Museum (NASM 2009-22214), 21; George Rinhart/Corbis/Getty Images, 23; Keystone-France/Gamma-Rapho/Getty Images, 26; ullstein bild/Getty Images, 28–29; Sueddeutsche Zeitung Photo/Alamy, 31; Interfoto/Alamy, 32; Bettmann/Getty Images, 38; AP Images, 40–41, 69, 83; Planet News Archive/SSPL/Getty Images, 44; Leonard McCombe/Picture Post/Hulton Archive/Getty Images, 48; iStockphoto, 50–51; Red Line Editorial, 51, 75; Agentur Voller Ernst/picture-alliance/dpa/AP Images, 52–53; AFP Photo/Ria Novosti/Getty Images, 55; Sputnik/Alamy, 58; Sovfoto/UIG/Getty Images, 60–61; Smithsonian National Air and Space Museum (NASM 2003-7208), 72; PhotoQuest/Getty Images, 76; Smithsonian National Air and Space Museum (NASM 2009-30142), 86 (bottom); Kent Media/REX Shutterstock/Rex Features/AP Images, 93; Pete Souza/White House, 95

Editor: Kate Conley
Series Designer: Maggie Villaume

PUBLISHER'S CATALOGING-IN-PUBLICATION DATA

Names: Moore, Shannon Baker, author.
Title: Women with wings: women pilots of World War II / by Shannon Baker Moore.
Other titles: Women pilots of World War II
Description: Minneapolis, MN : Abdo Publishing, 2017. | Series: Hidden heroes | Includes bibliographical references and index.
Identifiers: LCCN 2016945474 | ISBN 9781680783919 (lib. bdg.) | ISBN 9781680797442 (ebook)
Subjects: LCSH: World War, 1939-1945--Aerial operations--Juvenile literature. | World War, 1939-1945--Participation, Female--Juvenile literature. | Women air pilots--History--20th century--Juvenile literature.
Classification: DDC 940.54--dc23
LC record available at http://lccn.loc.gov/2016945474

CONTENTS

CHAPTER ONE

"TRAIN TWO WOMEN TO FLY IT"

Dora Dougherty climbed into the cockpit of the B-29 bomber, with copilot Dorothea "Didi" Johnson right beside her. The two women had never flown a four-engine bomber before, but they were determined to learn. This airplane, the Boeing B-29 Superfortress, was the most powerful bomber of World War II (1939–1945). It had 12 machine guns, one cannon, and a maximum bomb load of 20,000 pounds (9,071 kg).[1] It also had a dangerous reputation.

The B-29's first test flight happened on September 21, 1942. It had gone smoothly.

Dora Dougherty flew nearly every type of army aircraft.

However, the second test flight, on February 18, 1943, ended in disaster. Fuel leaked inside a wing and then caught on fire. The blaze spread to the engines. The plane lost power, crashed into a nearby factory, and burst into flames. All 11 crew members, including Boeing's chief test pilot, were killed. Twenty factory workers and a local firefighter also died.

As a result of the crash, many air force pilots refused to fly the B-29. As far as they were concerned, the aircraft was a death trap with unreliable engines, habitual fires, and inadequate testing. Dougherty and Johnson, two female aviators who were Women Airforce Service Pilots (WASPs), had a different opinion. They jumped at the chance

THE US AIR FORCE

In the early days of flight, air power was part of the US Army. A pilot's main job was to support troops on the ground. As planes improved, air power became an important part of war. Planes could be used for missions such as surveillance or bombing. When the United States entered World War II, the army's air units became the Army Air Forces (AAF). The AAF officially became the US Air Force in 1947.

A year later, women were allowed to join the air force. They could only perform ground duties, however, such as operating radar, reporting weather conditions, or nursing patients. The military changed its policies in 1976, and from then on, women could join the US Air Force as pilots. They could not fly in combat, however, until 1993. Today, more than 62,000 women serve in the US Air Force.[2] They are pilots, navigators, and mechanics.

The B-29s were put into production before all testing was completed, so the army set up modification centers where last-minute alterations could be made to the aircraft.

to learn to fly such an impressive plane. "We thought it was a great opportunity for us," said Dougherty. "We wanted to be part of the effort of proving this plane in any way we could."[3]

Tibbets's Plan

The United States and its allies desperately needed the B-29 Superfortress in the skies to win World War II. It had many advantages. The Superfortress could hold enough fuel to fly long distances, which was critical for long-range bombing missions. It also flew 30 percent faster than other bombers, and it had a pressurized cabin so it could fly at high altitudes.[4]

The Army Air Forces needed to convince male pilots the B-29 was safe. That job fell to Paul Tibbets. Tibbets had approximately 1,000 flying hours in the B-29, and he knew it could be flown safely. He just needed to figure out how to prove it to other pilots. Then Tibbets had an idea. According to Tibbets, he heard "they were having trouble at the [airbase] in Clovis, New Mexico, trying to get college football heroes to fly the B-29. . . . Didn't take me long to figure it out. What would you do? I said, train two women to fly it."[5]

At that point, Tibbets recruited Dougherty and Johnson to train on the B-29. As WASPs, Dougherty and Johnson were licensed pilots who flew US military airplanes during World War II. When Tibbets approached them in 1944, they were both stationed at Eglin Air Force Base in Florida. They flew planes that towed targets for aerial shooting practice.

Despite their training, neither WASP had flown a four-engine plane before. In fact, Dougherty, who was five feet five inches tall (165 cm), wasn't even sure she was big enough to handle such a large aircraft. But Dougherty was excited to learn. "We realized why they had us fly it," said Dougherty, "showing how

"Our heroes back then weren't movie stars and rock stars. Our heroes were the people who were pushing back the frontiers in the sky, people who had made headlines, gone faster, gone farther."[6]

—Dora Dougherty, WASP

easy it was to fly that even a girl could do it. We didn't feel bad about that."[7]

Training on the B-29

Dougherty and Johnson left Eglin Air Force Base and traveled to Birmingham, Alabama. Tibbets chose Birmingham because it had a large modification center where workers outfitted B-29s for the war. The center always had many B-29s in stock, so Tibbets knew that if one plane broke down during training, they would have access to another one right way. Tibbets hoped this supply of B-29s would allow the training to go quickly and without interruption.

In May 1944, the two WASPs began their training with Tibbets and flight

DORA DOUGHERTY

Dora Dougherty was born in Saint Paul, Minnesota, in 1921. Her love of flying started early, when her family would go to the airport on Sundays after church. There, the family spent time watching planes take off and land.

Dougherty's interest in flying grew. After her first year of college, she signed up for the Civilian Pilot Training Program (CPTP) and learned to fly. "It was a thrill. . . . I think that a lot of the excitement is that it's something new, that you're in control and that the success of the flight depends on you," she said.[8]

After flying with WASPs in World War II, Dougherty earned a doctorate in aviation education and psychology. She went on to work at Bell Helicopter, and later broke helicopter records for distance and altitude. Dougherty died in 2013, but her legacy in women's aviation lives on.

engineer Wyatt Dusenberry. The training was intense. The cockpit of the B-29 bomber was scorching hot under the Alabama sun. It got so hot the pilots needed gloves so they wouldn't burn their hands on the controls. The B-29 had no hydraulic controls, so it took a great deal of physical strength to control it. It was hard, hot work, and Dougherty was drenched in sweat as she maneuvered the plane.

For three days straight, seven hours a day, Dougherty practiced maneuvering the plane. Tibbets taught her what to do if an engine stopped running and how to take off with only two engines. Tibbets also made sure Dougherty knew how to pull the B-29 out of a stall. This dangerous situation happens when an aircraft's wings don't have enough lift to keep it in the air, often leading to a crash. With an aircraft as large as the B-29, pulling out of a stall was difficult, but Dougherty mastered it. She was an excellent student, and according to Tibbets, he could "show her something one time and she could repeat it."[9]

Dougherty even got to experience how to handle an onboard fire. On the first day of training, the cockpit filled with smoke. Her number three engine was on fire. The flight engineer looked to Tibbets through the smoke, thinking he would take command of the aircraft. Tibbets told the engineer to wait and see what Dougherty would

Dorothea "Didi" Johnson, *left*, Paul Tibbets, *center*, and Dora Dougherty, *right*, stand in front of *Ladybird*, the B-29 the women used for demonstration flights.

do. Calm and unflustered, she told the flight engineer to reduce the engine's drag to help the plane glide better and get out the fire extinguisher. She followed procedures precisely and landed the plane safely.

Changing Minds

After successfully finishing training, the two WASP B-29 pilots were ready to begin doing demonstration flights. They had "Ladybird" painted on the nose of the B-29 they flew, along with a picture of the WASP mascot, Fifinella. Then they took crews on demonstration flights to show them how to fly the B-29 bomber. Dougherty pointed out that these were "seasoned, four-engine combat crews," and Tibbets said that the crews were "dumbfounded" to see how the women flew the B-29.[10]

"You came to show us that the B-29 plane was not one to be feared. . . . I will admit that I was scared, even though I had just returned from flying B-24s in North Africa. You made the difference in my flying from then on."[11]

—Lieutenant Colonel Harry McKeown in a letter to Dora Dougherty

Tibbets's plan worked, and the women successfully gave many demonstration flights. A few weeks later, they received orders to stop. General Barney Giles had learned about the WASP demonstration flights, and he was unhappy about them.

FIFINELLA

Fifinella was the official WASP mascot. Author Roald Dahl created "fifinellas" as female gremlins in his book *The Gremlins*. In the story, mischievous gremlins tamper with airplanes. A British pilot convinces them to fight Germany's dictator, Adolf Hitler, instead of making mischief. They learn to repair planes instead of destroying them.

Walt Disney illustrated Dahl's book. In November 1942, a WASP named Byrd Howell Granger wrote to Walt Disney. She asked for permission to use Fifinella as the WASP official mascot. Disney agreed, and Fifinella was painted on planes, used in the WASP newsletter, *The Fifinella Gazette*, and worn as a patch on WASP flight jackets.

He said the female pilots were "putting the big football players to shame."[12]

With the demonstration flights over, Dougherty and Johnson returned to Eglin Air Force Base, and never again flew a B-29. But that did not matter. The two WASPs had accomplished their mission. These two women proved to hundreds of male pilots that the B-29 was not an airplane to be feared.

Leading the Way

Between 1942 and 1944, more than 1,000 WASPs flew noncombat military assignments throughout the United States. They flew every type of army aircraft available and logged more than 60 million miles (97 million km).[13] Female pilots ferried new aircraft from factories to military bases. They also worked as test pilots, flight instructors, and cargo transport pilots. Some towed targets attached to the back of their planes

FIFI

Many museums have B-29s on display. However, there is only one B-29 that is still flying today: *Fifi*. The plane is flown by a group called the Commemorative Air Force (CAF). Its pilots fly historic World War II planes in US air shows. They named the last flying B-29 *Fifi* in honor of Fifinella. The CAF rescued the historic B-29 in the early 1970s from a US Navy facility where it was being used for target practice.

while male pilots shot at the targets with live ammunition for shooting practice.

Though WASPs never fought in combat, their job was not without dangers. Thirty-eight WASPs died serving their country during World War II. Eleven of them died while in training. The remaining 27 were each on missions when they died in crashes caused by poor weather, engine fires, midair collisions, or equipment problems.

The women who flew as WASPs were only some of the female aviators who flew during World War II. Germany had a few female test pilots. The United Kingdom had female ferry pilots. Russia not only had women pilots, but it also had all-female combat squadrons.

Motivated by patriotism and a love of flying, these female pilots were pioneers, opening future opportunities for women. As Dougherty put it, "I think that, aside from the thrill of it, anytime that any of the women pilots flew anyplace, they felt they were representing women worldwide and for generations to come. We knew we were breaking barriers, and we had to fly our best."[14]

CHAPTER TWO

PIONEERS

In 1783, two Frenchmen captured the world's
attention when they became the first humans
to fly. Jean-François Pilâtre de Rozier and
his passenger, François Laurent, Marquis
d'Arlandes, took off from Paris, France, in a
hot air balloon. Unlike previous hot air balloon
rides, nothing tethered these men to the
ground. They floated freely above the city for
more than 20 minutes, covering a distance of
ten miles (16 km) before landing.[1]

In 1805, French woman Sophie Blanchard
became the first female to fly a hot air balloon.
She turned flying into a career, becoming the
first professional female balloonist. Blanchard
made long-distance flights from France to
Italy, and she even served King Louis XVIII as
an official flyer for France.

Sophie Blanchard stands in the basket of her
hot air balloon as she makes a flight in Milan,
Italy, in 1811.

Inventors soon began experimenting with other types of aircraft, such as gliders and airships. However, these were slow and hard to steer. It wasn't until Orville and Wilbur Wright's innovations that sustained, controllable heavier-than-air flight was possible. Through relentless study, testing, and persistence, they invented and built the first successful airplane. Its first flight was on December 17, 1903, in Kitty Hawk, North Carolina. That day, the Wright brothers made four flights, the longest lasting 59 seconds.[2]

The First Female Pilot

When Wilbur Wright arrived in France on August 8, 1908, to show off an airplane, he offered rides to ladies in the audience. One woman, Baroness Raymonde de la Roche, was already an accomplished balloonist. She wasn't going to miss a chance like this. Soon de la Roche was taking flying lessons herself.

On October 22, 1909, de la Roche flew over France, becoming the world's first female pilot. Less than a year later, she made history again. On March 10, 1910, de la Roche became the first woman ever to receive a pilot's license. Despite several serious crashes, de

"Flying does not rely so much on strength, as on physical and mental co-ordination."[3]

—Baroness de la Roche

On her first solo flight, Baroness de la Roche flew in a Voisin biplane for 984 feet (300 m).

la Roche was determined to stay in the skies. She traveled across Europe, demonstrating her flying skills.

American aviator Harriet Quimby was the world's second licensed female pilot. Inspired by an air show, Quimby began taking flying lessons in Long Island, New York. In 1911, she became the first American woman to earn a pilot's license. The next year, she became the first woman to fly solo across the English Channel.

The Golden Age of Flight

The 1920s and 1930s were known as the Golden Age of Flight. During these years, aviation expanded rapidly. Airpower became an essential part of military might.

Air races and record-breaking feats dominated the news. Daring pilots, such as Charles Lindbergh and Amelia Earhart, became celebrities.

For women, the Golden Age of Flight brought new opportunities. Some female aviators worked as sales pilots, demonstrating airplanes and selling them to private buyers. They proved effective at sales because at that time, many male buyers felt that if a woman could fly a plane, it must be easy. Other female pilots went into business for themselves, carrying passengers on sightseeing flights or teaching flying lessons.

Women also flew as stunt pilots during the Golden Age of Flight. They performed loops and dives, passed under bridges, and flew through barns. Some tricks required two people, one flying and another walking on the plane's wings or hanging beneath the plane. Ruth Law, the first

NETA SNOOK

Neta Snook fell in love with flying as a girl when she first saw hot air balloons at a county fair. In 1915, she applied to Curtiss Flying School in Virginia. Their answer? "No females allowed."[4] That did not stop Snook. After classes at two different flight schools, she learned to build her own plane, fly it, and repair it. After World War I (1914–1918), Snook moved to California and tested planes, ferried passengers, and gave flying lessons. Her most famous student was Amelia Earhart, who went on to make aviation history herself.

In addition to stunt flying, Ruth Law broke records for altitude and distance.

woman to loop-the-loop, created an air show called Ruth Law's Flying Circus. It traveled to local fairs, where Law raced against cars, flew through fireworks, and set speed records. For one of Law's most famous stunts, she climbed out of her cockpit and stood on the wing while her copilot did three loop-the-loops.

Obstacles

Female pilots faced the same problems as other women in male-dominated fields. In 1929, pilot Bruce Gould wrote about common attitudes toward female pilots. He said many male pilots considered women "by nature impulsive and scatter-brained."[5] These traits might lead a female pilot to ignore the airplane's controls, forget to fuel the plane, or fail to notice other planes in the sky. According to Gould, "women flyers will never excel, and rarely equal men in the air."[6]

Given these attitudes, finding a paying job as a pilot was difficult for women. Helen Richey became the first female commercial airline pilot when she accepted a job with Central Airways in 1934. She was an experienced pilot, but the company's male pilots refused to fly with her. They claimed Richey was too weak to fly in bad weather.

AIRPLANES IMPROVE

Early aircraft were simple biplanes made of wood and fabric. They had two wings on each side of an open cockpit. By the 1930s, airplanes had begun to change. New aircraft were monoplanes, with one large wing on each side of a closed cockpit. Metal monoplanes were stronger, faster, and sleeker than wooden biplanes.

Central Airlines dismissed the complaints about Richey, so the male pilots went to the Air Commerce Department. It oversaw all commercial flights, and its members sided with the male pilots. They ruled that female commercial pilots could fly only in good weather. Richey was so angry she quit in protest.

In her career, Helen Richey worked as a stunt pilot, commercial pilot, and ferry pilot in World War II.

Bessie Coleman

When Bessie Coleman wanted to take flying lessons, she faced even greater obstacles. US flying schools refused her not only because she was female, but also because she was African American. That didn't stop her. She traveled to France to take flying lessons and earned her pilot's license on June 15, 1921.

When Coleman returned to the United States, she became a barnstormer. She performed in front of both black and white audiences, and she insisted that there be no segregated gates at her shows. Coleman died in a plane crash in 1926, and three years later the Bessie Coleman Aero Club was named in her honor. The flight school trained many African-American pilots, until it closed in the early 1930s.

Racing in the Sky

Throughout the 1920s and 1930s, women displayed their skills by racing airplanes cross-country. The 1929 Women's Air Derby was the first official flying race for women. The starting point was in Santa Monica, California, and the race ended nine days later in Cleveland, Ohio.

To enter the race, each female pilot had to have completed at least 100 flying hours.[7] Each pilot also was required to fly an airplane with "appropriate" horsepower for a woman, which meant a plane that was not too fast. Racer Opal Kunz owned and routinely flew her 300-horsepower Travel Air plane, but she couldn't fly it in the race. It was considered "too fast for a woman to fly."[8] Kunz did not let that stop her, however, and she found another plane to fly in the race.

Nineteen planes took off on August 28, 1929, competing for a $25,000 prize.[9] On day two of the race, the favorite to win, Marvel Crosson, crashed in Arizona and was killed. Some considered canceling the race, but the pilots felt continuing the race would be a way to honor Crosson's memory. When pilot Louise Thaden landed in first place at the Cleveland airfield, crowds, reporters, and photographers swarmed her plane. Thaden dedicated her trophy to Crosson.

Making History

Following closely behind Thaden in the Women's Air Derby was another promising pilot, Amelia Earhart. In 1930, Earhart set the women's world speed record by flying at 181 miles per hour (291 kmh).[10] It wasn't long before she was making history again. In 1932, she took off from Newfoundland, flew across the Atlantic Ocean, and landed in a field in Ireland. This flight marked the first time a women had flown solo across the Atlantic

MYSTERIOUS DISAPPEARANCE

In 1937, Amelia Earhart and her navigator, Fred Noonan, tried to fly around the globe. They had successfully flown 22,000 miles (35,405 km) and had 7,000 miles (11,265 km) to go.[11] On July 2, 1937, they took off en route to Howland Island, a tiny Pacific Island less than 1 mile (1.6 km) wide and 2 miles (3.2 km) long.[12] Maps and navigation equipment were less accurate than today, and Earhart and Noonan got off course. They lost radio contact with a US Coast Guard ship stationed nearby, and the plane was never heard from again. Despite a 17-day search across 250,000 square miles (647,000 sq km), Earhart's plane could not be found.[13] The mystery of what happened to Earhart and Noonan continues to this day.

Well-wishers greeted Amelia Earhart in Londonderry, Ireland, after her flight across the Atlantic Ocean. It was the first solo transatlantic flight by a woman.

Ocean. She completed the flight in just 14 hours and 56 minutes.[14]

Like Earhart, other female pilots pushed the limits of aviation and broke more records. In 1936, Thaden and her copilot, Blanche Noyes, won the Bendix Transcontinental Air Race. They beat both male and female competitors. The Bendix Race had banned women from participating for several years, but they reopened the race to women in 1935.

Thaden never expected to win because she had ongoing problems during her flight. Shortly after takeoff, the two flyers realized their radio was out. They had no way to find out how far ahead or behind they were from other racers. Turbulent air in New Mexico also slowed them down.

When Thaden and Noyes finally got to Los Angeles, California, the afternoon sun was in their eyes. Because it was hard to see, the women crossed the finish line from the wrong direction. When they finally landed, they thought they had come in last. They were stunned when race officials told them they had won.

THE NINETY-NINES

In 1929, the United States had 117 licensed female pilots.[15] Twenty-six of them gathered in an airplane hangar on November 2, 1929, at Curtiss Field on Long Island, New York. They organized a club to promote female aviators. Membership was open to any woman with a pilot's license. They named their club for the number of charter members. They were the 86s, the 97s, and then finally the 99s. Today, the Ninety-Nines Organization still has members worldwide.

"If you have flown, perhaps you can understand the love a pilot develops for flight. It is much the same emotion a man feels for a woman, or a wife for her husband."[16]

—Louise Thaden

CHAPTER THREE

WAR IN THE SKIES

Military leaders began using aviation widely in World War I (1914–1918). Armies used airplanes to track enemy movements. Airplanes were unarmed, and enemy pilots would even wave to each other as they flew by. This friendship in the skies didn't last long. In 1915, the first fighter planes armed with machine guns appeared, along with airplanes used for bombing.

The usefulness of airplanes in warfare, grew as planes became larger, stronger, and faster. Runways, lighted beacons, air traffic rules, and improved instruments made flying safer.

A squadron of German planes flew over Berlin's Brandenburg Gate in 1939 to display the country's military force.

The Luftwaffe

The idea of using airplanes as weapons intensified in the years leading up to World War II. When Adolf Hitler became Germany's leader in 1933, he quickly set to work building an air force. The peace treaty signed after World War I forbid Germany from making warplanes, so Hitler ordered pilots to be trained secretly. Then in 1935, Hitler officially created Germany's air force, the Luftwaffe. At the time of its creation, it already had 1,800 aircraft and 20,000 officers.[1]

As the Luftwaffe grew, aviator Hanna Reitsch was working as a test pilot for the Glider Research Institute in Darmstadt, Germany. She tested a variety of gliders, as well as brakes used to slow a plane when it was in a dive. German officials realized the usefulness of the dive brakes and installed them on Luftwaffe aircraft. For her work, Reitsch became the first women to earn the title *Flugkapitän* (flight captain), and in 1937, she began working directly for the Luftwaffe as a test pilot.

> "My parents had shown me as a child the storks in their quiet and steady flight, the buzzards, circling ever higher in the summer air, and so, when I, too, expressed a longing to fly they took it as a childish fancy . . . . (But) it turned into a deep, insistent homesickness, a yearning that went with me everywhere and could never be stilled."[2]
>
> —Hanna Reitsch

Hanna Reitsch broke more than 40 world records for flying in gliders and airplanes during her career.

Luftwaffe leaders also turned to the talents of another woman, Melitta Schiller. Schiller was a physicist, flight engineer, and pilot. In 1936, she began working at an aviation company called Askania Werke in Berlin, Germany. Her research work there attracted the attention

Some days, Melitta Schiller performed more than 15 test dives. By the war's end, she had completed more than 2,500 dives.

of the government, and like Reitsch, Schiller began working as a test pilot for the Luftwaffe.

Schiller and Reitsch forged an unusual path for women in Germany during the late 1930s. German laws required most women to quit their jobs, especially if they were married. Not only were Schiller and Reitsch allowed to keep working, but they also had the rare position of working in the male-dominated military. They received this special treatment because German leaders wanted to use the women's skill and knowledge to their advantage in the impending war.

Training Civilians

The world watched with uneasiness as Hitler built his military. In the United States, leaders began to prepare for a possible war. On June 27, 1939, President Franklin D. Roosevelt approved the

DIFFERENT VIEWS

Though Hanna Reitsch and Melitta Schiller are often linked together as German test pilots, they had very different views of the war. Reitsch was patriotic, strongly supporting Hitler and the Nazis. When it looked as if Germany would be defeated, Reitsch went so far as to create a suicide bombing squad for the Luftwaffe, though it was never put to use. Schiller, on the other hand, feared her future under Hitler. She was one-quarter Jewish, and had successfully hidden that fact to save herself. Schiller worked secretly with her husband, Alexander von Stauffenberg, and his brother Claus in a plot to assassinate Hitler. The plot failed, and officials never learned of Schiller's role in it.

Civilian Pilot Training Program (CPTP). Its goal was to create a large pool of trained civilian pilots in case the air force needed more pilots. More than 400 US colleges offered CPTP classes, and one woman was allowed for every ten male students.[3] Students paid $40 to attend the program, which included 72 hours of ground school and 35–50 hours of flight time.[4]

As US involvement in the war looked more likely, the CPTP began to require all graduating pilots to join the military. Since women could not enlist as combat pilots, the CPTP stopped offering classes to women in June 1941. While the program had not lasted long, it was a resounding success for female pilots. Before the CPTP began, only 675 American women had pilot's licenses.[5] When the program ended, more than 3,000 women had earned their licenses.[6]

THE CPTP'S DIVERSITY

When President Roosevelt signed the Civilian Pilot Training Act into law, it included a section that said that "none of the benefits of training or programs shall be denied on account of race, creed, or color."[7] As a result, more women and African Americans received flight training than ever before. When the program ended in 1944, it had trained more than 435,000 pilots.[8]

World War II Begins

On September 1, 1939, German forces invaded Poland. The Luftwaffe played a major role in the invasion, as its 1,300 warplanes downed communication lines, bombed airfields, and damaged cities.[9] The Luftwaffe, along with more than 1.5 million German soldiers, overwhelmed Polish forces that were not as well equipped. The invasion outraged many world leaders, and on September 3, the United Kingdom and France declared war on Germany. World War II had officially begun.

German troops marched across Europe throughout 1940, occupying Denmark, the Netherlands, Belgium, and France. Hitler's next target was the United Kingdom. The Battle of Britain began in July 1940, when German leaders sent thousands of aircraft to destroy the British Royal Air Force (RAF) and its air bases.[10] Air attacks grew especially fierce beginning on September 7, 1940, when the Germans dropped bombs on London, England, for 57 nights in a row.[11]

At first, it looked like Germany might win, but the RAF grew stronger and more skilled. It had the world's most advanced radar system, which reduced the element of surprise during attacks. The RAF pilots also used fighter planes that were smaller and lighter, and which could turn and dodge more quickly than the bulkier German planes. The heavier German planes also had to refuel more often. By June 1941, Hitler realized his plan wasn't working, and he began focusing more attacks on the Soviet Union.

Pearl Harbor

The United States hoped to stay out of World War II. Although the United States sold the United Kingdom and the Soviet Union war supplies, American soldiers were not directly involved in combat at the start of the war. However, that all changed on the morning of December 7, 1941, when Japan, one of Germany's allies, led a surprise attack on Pearl Harbor, Hawaii.

On that morning, civilian pilot Cornelia Fort was giving a flying lesson to one of her students near Pearl Harbor. They were practicing takeoffs and landings. On the last landing, Fort glanced around and saw a plane coming directly toward her. Fort said, "I jerked the controls away from my student and jammed the throttle wide open to pull above the oncoming plane. He passed so close under us that our . . . windows rattled violently and I looked down to see what kind of plane it was. The painted red balls on the tops of the wings shone brightly in the sun."[12]

Fort had spotted a Japanese fighter plane. She looked again and the sky was full of bombers flying in. She saw bombs falling and exploding in Pearl Harbor, which was home to the US Navy's Pacific Fleet. "I set about landing

After the attack on Pearl Harbor, Cornelia Fort returned to the US mainland and taught flight lessons as part of the CPTP.

as quickly as ever I could," said Fort. "A few seconds later a shadow passed over me and simultaneously bullets spattered all around me."[13]

On December 8, just one day after the attack on Pearl Harbor that Fort had witnessed, the United States declared war on Japan. Three days later, the United States declared war on Germany. The United States had officially joined the Allied forces, and it began sending soldiers

By training women, the US military lessened the nation's massive pilot shortage.

into combat. The military needed thousands of pilots. Most qualified male pilots were sent to war as combat pilots. Noncombat piloting jobs, such as ferrying planes and providing training, remained unfilled. With the men off at war, female pilots filled these jobs and began flying for the military for the first time.

All kinds of different women served as pilots during World War II: barnstormers, dancers, college graduates, wives, farmers, and high-society women. One thing united these women: they loved to fly. Many were also motivated by a love of their country. It was a unique time and a unique chance to prove themselves as pilots and as patriots.

PILOT SHORTAGE

When the United States joined World War II, its troops began fighting on two fronts: Europe and the Pacific. Military leaders quickly realized they needed large numbers of trained pilots to win the war. In December 1941, the military's goal was to have 50,000 trained pilots. By the fall of 1942, that number had risen to 102,000.[14] More than doubling the number of US pilots needed in less than a year had created a shortage. To solve the problem, the military eased the requirements for becoming a pilot. Pilots no longer needed to be single or have two years of college, and the minimum age to serve dropped from 21 to 18. The military also turned to female pilots, an idea that had met resistance in the past when the need for pilots had been less urgent.

CHAPTER FOUR
"ATA-GIRLS"

In the United Kingdom, women flew in the Women's Section of the Air Transport Auxiliary (ATA). The ATA was the idea of Sir Gerard d'Erlanger, a pilot and eventual director of British Airways. In September 1938, many Europeans saw war coming, including d'Erlanger. The RAF was tiny and ill-prepared compared to the German air force. D'Erlanger suggested the RAF used civilian pilots to fly noncombat missions, such as delivering mail and supplies.

On September 3, 1939, the United Kingdom declared war on Germany, and the ATA began with 30 men.[1] ATA pilots did not meet the qualifications needed to fly for the RAF. Some ATA pilots wore glasses, some were color-blind, some were too old, and

Members of the first group of female ATA pilots prepared to ferry RAF trainer planes from the factory to air bases.

some had only one arm or one eye. As a result, some people joked that ATA stood for "Ancient and Tattered Airmen." But the jokes didn't stop the ATA from its important work, such as delivering airplanes from factories to the combat airfields, where they were fitted with guns and radios.

Early in the war, the United Kingdom had more planes than pilots. These extra planes were parked at airfields and were prime targets for German bombers. The ATA desperately needed more pilots and considered hiring women, but it was a controversial decision. People disagreed as to whether women should—or even could—fly. As one male ATA pilot put it years later, "Well I suppose today you wouldn't understand it because women are doing the same thing as men all round. But in those days. . . . the idea

AMY JOHNSON

In May 1928, British pilot Amy Johnson flew solo from England to Australia in just 19 and a half days. She became an instant celebrity. Johnson was a flier who focused on setting records; she and her husband became the first husband-and-wife team to cross the Atlantic Ocean from east to west. Johnson joined the ATA in March 1940. She died in January 1941, when she took off on an ATA flight in cloudy weather. With no opening in the cloud cover, Johnson could not descend. She bailed out of her plane over the Thames Estuary, where she drowned.

of them being an equal of men at flying—it was a bit revolutionary."[2]

Pauline Gower

Pauline Gower, an experienced British pilot, knew women could play an important role in wartime aviation, and she worked tirelessly to promote the cause of female fliers. Gower had grown up as the

> "Women are not born with wings, neither are men for that matter. Wings are won by hard work, just as proficiency is won in any profession."[3]
>
> —Pauline Gower

youngest daughter of a well-to-do family, and her father was a member of Parliament. As a young woman, she tried to figure out what to do with her life. She studied all kinds of subjects: music, mythology, photography, horseback riding, and politics. Then she went on her first airplane ride, and she was hooked. Gower wanted to be a pilot.

Gower's father thought aviation was an inappropriate choice for his daughter, and he refused to pay for her flying lessons. That didn't stop Gower. She raised the money herself by teaching violin lessons. After just seven hours of flight instruction, she made her first solo flight. She earned her pilot's license in August 1930.

Flying became a central part of Gower's life. She joined an airplane club and made friends with other female

Pauline Gower used the connections of her father, Sir Robert Gower, to help start the women's division of the ATA.

aviators. She learned how to fly at night and also worked as a joyrider, taking customers on airplane rides.

Eventually, Gower and her father made up. On Gower's twenty-first birthday, he gave her a used two-seater plane. Gower flew for an air circus, ran an air taxi service, and worked on government aviation committees. Given her social status and her father's political connections, Gower was well positioned to help push for female pilots. In December 1939, the ATA assigned Gower to organize its women's section of pilots.

The Lucky Eight

Gower had permission to start with only eight pilots. Well acquainted with many skilled female pilots, Gower flight-tested her top twelve, and then selected the lucky eight. They began their service in January 1940. The Women's Section had provisional status, which meant that it was considered a test program. The women had to prove that they could safely handle heavy aircraft.

THE EIGHT ORIGINALS

The eight original members of the ATA Women's Section were not only accomplished pilots; but were also accomplished in other fields. Rosemary Rees de Cros, for example, had been a professional dancer, and Margaret Fairweather was a trained singer. Marion Wilberforce was a farmer, and Mona Friedlander was an international ice hockey player.

Women who wanted to join the ATA had to be at least five feet five inches (1.65 m) tall. This ensured the pilots were tall enough to reach the pedals and see out of the cockpit window. Pilots had to be between 22 and 45 years old and have at least 500 hours of solo flight time.[4]

The female pilots became known as the "ATA-Girls," and they got a lot of publicity. Sometimes it gave a completely inaccurate picture of the life of a female pilot. For instance, one newspaper photo posed the women in their ATA uniforms seated around linen-draped tables having tea beside the airfield.

As the war dragged on and the United Kingdom grew more desperate for pilots, the requirements were lowered. In early 1943, the pilot shortage was so bad that women were allowed to join even if they had no flying time. They would be trained to fly. The ATA accepted female pilots from 25 other countries, too.[7] Many of these women flew for the United Kingdom because their countries did not allow women to fly in the military.

"(T)here were thousands of applications (for the women's section). ATA could afford to be choosy, and they were."[8]

—Rosemary Rees du Cros,
ATA pilot

Flying as an ATA Pilot

Flying for the ATA was challenging. When in the air, ATA pilots had no communication with the ground. They could not use radios, because radio frequencies were for combat pilots only. ATA pilots navigated by using a compass and tracking their route on a map. The ATA pilots had to fly below the clouds so they could see landmarks on the ground. They used railway lines, roads, and even clumps of trees as markers to help them find their way.

These flying conditions made the work of ATA pilots dangerous. It was easy to get lost, even with a map and compass. Airfields were camouflaged, making it hard to find where to land. Worst of all was weather that could turn stormy at a moment's notice. If pilots got caught above the clouds and couldn't find a hole in the clouds to

Female ATA pilots meet in a briefing room to learn of their next ferrying missions.

descend through, they might be forced to fly until they ran out of fuel and crashed.

Originally, the ATA allowed women to ferry only light aircraft, such as Tiger Moths. By May 1940, Gower had convinced the ATA to let the most experienced female pilots take courses to learn how to fly larger aircraft. By the end of the war, women were flying everything from Spitfire fighter planes to the huge four-engine Lancaster bombers. When ATA pilot Marion Wilberforce ended her service in 1945, she had flown 2,400 hours for the war effort and had experience in more than 100 different aircraft types.[9]

SPITFIRES

During World War II, the Spitfire was the most important fighter plane the RAF used. It was an all-metal, single-seater fighter with a closed cockpit and a distinctive elliptical-shaped wing. Early-model Spitfires could fly at up to 360 miles per hour (580 kmh). Later models could fly as fast as 440 miles per hour (710 kmh). The RAF began using Spitfires in 1938. Because the Spitfire was so quick and easy to maneuver, it could easily out turn German fighters. As a result, it was one of the most popular Allied fighter planes of World War II.

ABLE TO FLY ANYTHING

Each day, an ATA pilot could be called upon to fly one of 147 different aircraft.[10] The ATA classified planes into six different classes. Pilots who were certified to fly a Class 1 aircraft, for example, could fly any of the 12 planes in that class. Even within one model of plane, however, there could be many variations as the war progressed. Each variation operated a little differently, and the pilots could be called upon to fly any of them. Pilots used the Ferry Pilots Notes as a kind of "cheat-sheet" to help them fly any ATA aircraft. Ferry Pilots Notes were a flip pad of notecards covered on both sides with all the basic rules for flying each type of aircraft.

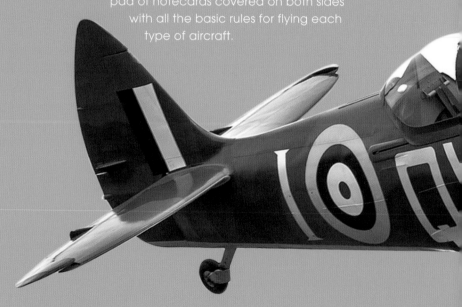

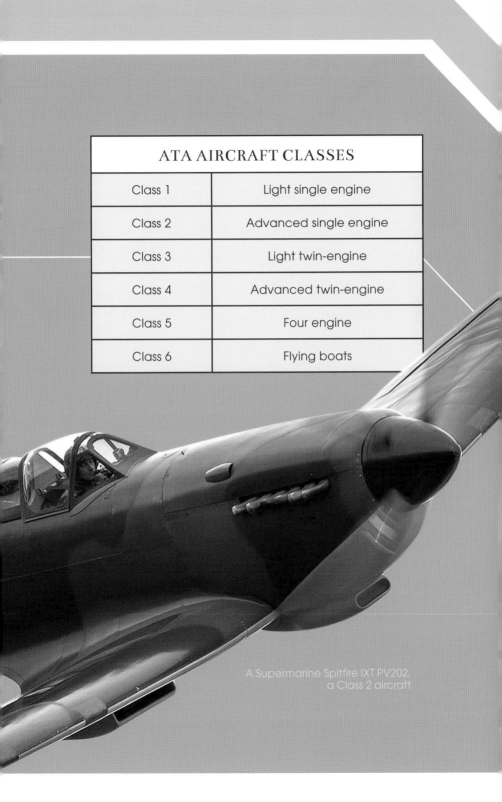

ATA AIRCRAFT CLASSES	
Class 1	Light single engine
Class 2	Advanced single engine
Class 3	Light twin-engine
Class 4	Advanced twin-engine
Class 5	Four engine
Class 6	Flying boats

A Supermarine Spitfire IXT PV202, a Class 2 aircraft.

CHAPTER FIVE

SOVIET PILOTS

As World War II continued, German forces pushed further east. On June 22, 1941, Germany invaded the Soviet Union. The invasion, called Operation Barbarossa, rapidly pushed into Soviet territory. By the end of 1941, German forces neared the Soviet capital, Moscow. The Germans also crippled the Soviet Air Force by destroying 8,000 Soviet planes.[1]

Like the United States, the Soviet Union had offered flight training to civilians in an effort to prepare for war. By 1941, between one-quarter and one-third of Soviet pilots were female. When the Germans attacked, these female pilots rushed to volunteer. At first, the Soviet military turned them down because it had not originally considered

Fighter pilot Yekaterina Ryabova was honored with a 1945 victory parade in Moscow. In the war she flew 860 night bombing missions.

women for military flying. But women were already serving in the Soviet Army, and the speed of the German invasion caused Soviet leaders to reconsider.

Marina Raskova

Pilot Marina Raskova was one of the people who worked tirelessly to convince Soviet leader Joseph Stalin that women should fly in military units. Raskova had a strong background as an aviator. She was the first woman in the Soviet Union to become a professional airplane navigator. Raskova also worked as a flight instructor, flew in air shows, and competed in air races.

Raskova had become famous for a flight she took in September 1938. Raskova and two other female pilots, Polina Osipenko and Valentina Grizodubova, flew from Moscow to Komsomolsk.

Marina Raskova commanded a regiment until her death in a 1943 plane crash.

As they reached the end of their flight, they didn't have enough fuel to make it to their planned destination. They had to make an emergency crash landing. Raskova bailed out of the plane and parachuted to the swamp below. She was lost for ten days.

After a search and rescue team recovered the pilots, they returned to Moscow as heroes. They had set a distance record of 4,008 miles (6,450 km), and they were treated like celebrities.[5] Raskova and her two fellow pilots received the Hero of the Soviet Union and the Order of

Lenin, two prestigious honors. Stalin also gave a banquet in their honor.

Female Fliers

Raskova used her connection with Stalin to convince him to create a women's flying program. On October 8, 1941, Raskova received permission to organize an all-female flight group. It had three regiments: the 586th Fighter Regiment, the 587th Dive Bomber Regiment, and the 588th Night Bombers. The 586th and 587th units eventually included a few men, but the 588th remained all-female for the entire war. Roughly 1,000 women served in these units.[6]

Many of these women had personal reasons for wanting to fight. Pilot Dusia Nosal's baby was killed in a bombing at the beginning of the war. Other women had lost their entire families in the war. Valentina Grizodubova said, "To avenge the dead, to assure a better future for the living—that is why we Russian women went up to battle the Nazi foe."[7]

In the fall of 1941, the first female pilots traveled

ONE MILLION WOMEN

During World War II, nearly one million Soviet women fought in the military and performed combat duties. In the United States, by contrast, just 350,000 served in the US military, and these were in noncombat positions.[8] Soviet women fought as pilots, sharpshooters, and tank commanders.

to Engels Air Force Base near Saratov, Russia. Their training was intense. They had to learn three years of flight training in only six months. Students took ten classes a day and had two hours of drills. Those students who would become navigators studied Morse code for an extra hour.

In addition to classes, daily life was hard. Sometimes they marched in the middle of the night, their coats pulled over their nightgowns. And the weather was bitter cold, with temperatures dropping as low as -4 degrees Fahrenheit (-20°C).[9] Despite the cold, the women flew in open-cockpit planes called Polikarpovs, nicknamed Po-2s.

The 586th Fighter Regiment

With training completed, the three regiments became active in 1942. The main mission of the 586th Fighter Regiment was defensive. They protected essential

Pilots of the 586th Regiment prepare a plane for a combat mission.

infrastructure, such as communication lines, factories, and railroads. They guarded military supplies and protected advancing ground troops. They flew in Yak fighter planes, and their activities extended west all the way to Vienna, Austria.

One of the regiment's most famous female fighter pilots was Lydia Litvyak. She was a daredevil flier, and after a successful mission, she would zoom in low over the airfield and do acrobatics. On

"You cannot judge by appearance. I know girls so quiet and apparently timid that they blush when spoken to, yet they pilot bombers over Germany without qualm. No country at war today can afford to ignore the tremendous reservoir of woman power."[11]

—Soviet pilot
Valentina Grizodubova

September 13, 1942, Litvyak shot down two enemy fighters on her very first mission.

One of the men Litvyak shot down was Erwin Maier, a German pilot who had shot down 11 planes. Maier parachuted from his plane and was captured by the Soviets. During questioning, Maier asked to meet the pilot who had shot him down. When Litvyak entered the room, he thought it was a joke. He didn't believe she had actually shot him down. So Litvyak proved it by describing every detail of their dogfight. He was forced to accept defeat. During her years as a pilot, Litvyak shot down 14 planes.[12] In August 1943, Litvyak's plane was shot down in an air battle against German planes, and she was never seen again.

The 587th Bomber Regiment

The 587th Bomber Regiment worked as dive bombers, attacking the enemy's camps and other strongholds. Flying in fast, twin-engine Pe-2 dive bombers, each pilot flew up to three bombing missions per day. By the end of the war, they had dropped more than 1,080 short tons (980 metric tons) of bombs.[13]

Raskova commanded the 587th Regiment until her death in an airplane crash in January 1943. Then a man named Valentin Markov took her place. At first, Markov was humiliated to be leading a group of female pilots.

The night witches of the 588th Regiment receive orders for an upcoming raid in 1944.

After working with them for a few months, however, his attitude changed. He realized what skilled pilots the women were, and he began to respect them.

The pilots of the 587th showed great courage in battle. Galina Dzhunkovskaya, for example, was caught in a gunfight with German fighters. She had run out of ammunition and the Germans were on her tail, ready to take her down. At the last moment, she took out a flare gun and shot it. The Germans thought the exploding flare was an aerial grenade, and they fled. In the spring of 1944, the plane Dzhunkovskaya was flying was hit and

the engine caught fire. She bailed from the plane and was
believed to be dead. In reality, friendly troops had picked
her up and helped her back to her base, where everyone
was amazed she had survived.

The 588th Night Bomber Regiment

Of the three female Soviet regiments, the best known was
the 588th Night Bomber Regiment. These women flew
Po-2s, each plane carrying a pilot, a navigator, and up to
eight bombs. The Po-2 was lightweight, easy to fly, and
easy to land. Since it was made of canvas and plywood,

> "We were keen to show we could fight as well as, if not better than the men. When they first saw us, they didn't take us seriously. They called us silly girls who should still be playing with dolls. . . . But in six months, their attitude changed completely. In 1943 our regiment was the first in the division to be awarded the honor of becoming a Guards regiment."[16]
>
> —Irina Rakobolskaya, 588th Night Bomber Regiment

enemy bullets could easily ignite a Po-2, and many pilots were shot down in flames.

Using only compasses and maps, the women of the 588th flew in open-cockpit planes at night in bitterly cold weather. The whooshing sounds the Po-2s made reminded German soldiers of a witch's broom, and the Germans called these female bomber pilots *Nachthexen* or "night witches." Each pilot flew eight or more missions a night. Pilot Nadia Popova once flew 18 missions in a single night.[14] During the war, the night witches flew 30,000 missions, dropping 23,000 short tons (20,865 metric tons) of bombs.[15]

Night witch Mariya Smirnova described one disastrous mission when her squadron went to bomb a heavily protected area. She expected antiaircraft fire, but heard none. She realized that meant German fighter planes were coming to attack. The German fighter planes were far more advanced than the glider-like Po-2s. Searchlights scanned the sky, lighting up the Soviet aircraft. Four planes were shot down. They caught fire, falling from the sky and "burning like sheets of paper," as Smirnova put it.[17]

Roughly one-third of the Soviet women died in combat.[18] Soviet fighter pilot Alexei Maresyev praised the pilots of the 586th, 587th, and 588th Regiments, saying, "It is hardly possible to overestimate the contribution made by [Soviet] women to our victory over Nazism . . . many of them fell on the battlefield, having discharged their soldierly duty honorably. They had a zest for life; they wanted to study, to raise children, and to work hard, but when the need arose they faced danger and died without faltering."[19]

FEROCIOUS REPUTATION

Over the course of the war, the night witches earned a reputation as ferocious fighters. Rumors spread among German soldiers that the women received special pills and injections to give them excellent night vision. "We simply couldn't grasp that the Soviet airmen that caused us the greatest trouble were in fact women. These women feared nothing. They came night after night in their very slow biplanes, and for some periods they wouldn't give us any sleep at all," wrote German pilot Johannes Steinhoff in 1942.[20]

CHAPTER SIX

WAFS & WFTD

In the years leading up to World War II, the
US Army Air Forces grew rapidly. In 1939,
the military was training just 300 pilots per
year.[1] The head of the US Army Air Forces,
General Henry "Hap" Arnold, thought as
many as 100,000 pilots would be needed.[2]
Congress dramatically increased spending for
the US Army Air Forces in April 1939, giving
it half of the entire military budget.[3]

Female pilots wanted to serve their
country, too. Women were barred from
enlisting in the air force as pilots, but that
didn't mean they couldn't help as civilians.
Two women, Nancy Harkness Love and
Jacqueline Cochran, played a central role in
developing flying programs for civilian female
pilots to work with the air force. While they

Pilots receive instructions as part of their
training to ferry US military aircraft during
World War II.

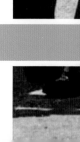

had different ideas about who should be pilots and how the programs should run, they each broke new ground for female pilots.

Nancy Love

Nancy Love was born in Houghton, Michigan, in 1914. She was inspired to fly after watching a barnstormer, and when she was 16 she became the youngest American woman to earn a private pilot's license. Love told her parents she wanted to quit school and become a pilot, but they insisted she go to college. She kept on flying and earned her commercial pilot's license while in college.

Love flew every chance she got. Her nickname was the "Flying Freshman," and she earned spending money by giving people airplane rides. One weekend, she took her date and another couple flying. They buzzed the campus, zipping by at treetop level. Someone reported their prank, and Love was kicked out of school for two weeks and banned from flying for the rest of the semester. That hardly slowed her down.

"Isn't there anything a girl of 23 can do in the event our country goes to war, except sit at home and become gray with worry? I learned to fly an airplane from a former World War ace. If only I were a man there would be a place for me."[4]

—From a young wife living in Queens, New York, in a 1941 letter that appeared in the New York Herald Tribune.

Before she was 20, she had logged 200 hours of flying time.[5]

In 1935, the US government hired Love and four other women pilots to airmark the United States. They traveled across the United States, flying over 16,000 towns and cities, on the lookout for rooftops that could be marked so they would be visible from the air. These air marks served as landmarks to help pilots navigate.[6]

Love served the United States in other ways, too. In 1940, she ferried airplanes to Canada, where they awaited shipment to France. Though France fell to the Germans before the planes arrived there, Love saw the potential for women to help in the war effort as ferry pilots.

Love's Idea

Love worked at the US Army Air Transport Command (ATC). It managed aircraft, aircrews, and military personnel all over the world. Love saw the massive need for pilots, and she knew there were many outstanding female fliers who would jump at the chance to ferry

FERRY PILOTS NEEDED

When the United States joined the war in 1941, airplane production swelled. Only 2,141 had been built in 1939, but by 1944, that number had expanded to 96,318.[7] As these planes came off the assembly line, they needed to be ferried to air force bases around the country. Most of the male pilots were overseas, fighting in the war. Experienced female pilots were the solution to this problem.

airplanes. She wanted to build an elite squadron of women who were already superior pilots and ready for duty.

In May 1940, Love wrote to Lieutenant Colonel Robert Olds and included a list of 49 female pilots who were excellent candidates. "I really think this list is up to handling pretty complicated stuff," Love wrote.[8] She also mentioned that there were probably even more who would also be well qualified. Olds was interested, but nothing happened.

Then, in 1942, Colonel William Tunner received the task of finding more pilots. Love presented her idea of female ferry pilots to Tunner. With Tunner's help, Love's idea became a reality. On September 10, 1942, Secretary of War Henry L. Stimson officially announced the formation of the Women's Auxiliary Ferrying Squadron (WAFS). The women would be hired as civilian employees, and they would be paid $250 a month as ferry pilots.[9]

WAFS Pilots

Love immediately began searching for pilots for her WAFS program. She sent telegrams to 83 female pilots, asking them to

FIRST MISSION

The WAFS undertook their first mission on October 22–23, 1942. WAFS pilots ferried six L-4B Piper Cubs from the factory in Pennsylvania to Mitchel Field in Long Island, New York.

Nancy Love and Colonel Robert H. Baker inspected the first class of WAFS at the New Castle Army Air Base.

serve in the Ferry Squadron. On September 21, 1942, the first pilots were sworn in at New Castle Army Air Base in Wilmington, Delaware. A total of 28 women were part of this first group. They were nicknamed "The Originals" because they were the first American women to fly military planes. They were also some of the most skilled, experienced pilots in the United States—male or female—with an average of 1,100 flying hours.[10]

Even with all their experience, the pilots required four weeks of flight training so they could learn to fly "the Army way." They took four weeks of classes, studying navigation, ferry routes, military terms, and ferry paperwork. They also tracked when the sun set each day because the Ferry Squadron wanted every plane on the ground by dark.

At first, women were approved to fly only light trainer planes, such as Piper Cubs and PT-19s, even though they were used to flying heavier planes with stronger engines. Soon they were allowed to ferry larger aircraft such as the P-38 Lightning and the P-51 Mustang. In fact, Love was one of the first pilots, male or female, to ever fly the P-51, a fighter that could fly at up to 440 miles per hour (708 kmh).[11]

Jacqueline Cochran

Love was not the only person pushing to use women as ferry pilots during the war. Pilot Jacqueline Cochran was also thinking of how useful female pilots could be for the military. Unlike Love, Cochran did not become interested in flying until she was an adult. At a party in 1932 she met millionaire Floyd Odlum. It was a meeting that would change her life and the future of women pilots.

As Odlum and Cochran talked, she described her dream of starting a cosmetics company. Her plans were so elaborate that he told her she'd need wings to be able to get it all done. Odlum then bet her she couldn't learn to fly in six weeks. She did it in three. Soon she was competing in air races. In 1937, she won first place in the women's division of the Bendix Air Race. She also won her first Harmon International trophy for breaking a speed record. In 1938, she won two more major awards. She had only been flying for five years.

Cochran's Idea

On September 28, 1939, less than a month after Germany attacked Poland, Cochran wrote a letter to First Lady Eleanor Roosevelt. In it, Cochran promoted the idea of an all-women ferrying group. Though Roosevelt supported the idea, nothing ever came of it. Then, in 1941, Cochran met General Arnold at a ceremony in Washington, DC. Cochran urged Arnold to establish an air force flying program for women. Arnold was hesitant, but Cochran was persistent.

> "It seems to me that in the Civil Air Patrol and in our own ferry command, women, if they can pass the tests imposed upon men, should have an equal opportunity for non-combat service. . . . This is not a time when women should be patient. We are in a war and we need to fight it with all our ability and every weapon possible. Women pilots, in this particular case, are a weapon waiting to be used."[12]
>
> —*Eleanor Roosevelt in her column My Day, September 1, 1942*

Arnold suggested she test her idea by organizing a group of American female pilots to fly for the British ATA. He added that planes and pilots were desperately needed in the United Kingdom, and offered Cochran the chance to be the first woman to fly a bomber there. On

Jacqueline Cochran wears her uniform as a flight captain for the British ATA in 1942.

June 17, 1941, Jackie Cochran flew a Lockheed Hudson bomber across the Atlantic.

In the spring of 1942, Cochran's plan was put into action. Twenty-five American women met the initial flight tests and physicals for the British ATA. The 24 who passed the final ATA physical journeyed to England and signed an 18-month contract to fly for the ATA. Cochran spent most of this time in London.

The WFTD

Cochran was in London when she learned the US military was about to announce a female ferrying program with Nancy Love as its leader. Within 24 hours, Cochran was on a flight back to the United States. Cochran returned on September 10, the same day Stimson announced Love's WAFS program.

On September 11, Cochran was back in General Arnold's office. The furious, strong-willed Cochran won out. On September 15, Secretary Stimson announced a second program for women pilots: the Women's Flying Training Detachment (WFTD). Cochran would be the program's director, responsible for training 500 female pilots.[13]

Cochran chose Howard Hughes Field in Houston, Texas, as a base for the WFTD program. She

FLYING REQUIREMENTS

Pilots for WAFS and the WFTD needed to meet many of the same requirements. They had to be US citizens, high school graduates, between 21 and 35 years old, and at least five feet (1.5 m) tall. But that is where the similarities ended. Cochran believed any pilot could be trained to fly military aircraft, and she required 200 flying hours to apply for the program.[14] Love wanted the WAFS to be a group of experienced, elite pilots. She required 500 flying hours, two letters of recommendation, a commercial pilot's license, and certification to fly at least a 200-horsepower-engine plane.[15]

sent applications to 150 women, and 130 replied. She personally interviewed each one and selected 30 for the first WFTD class.[16]

Training Begins

In November 1942, the 30 women paid their own way to Texas. Cochran told the women their work was classified and they should not tell others about it. She also told them not to expect fame or glory, just hard work. If women were ever going to be allowed to fly for the military, it was up to these women to prove it could work.

Every month, a new group arrived for training, and the WFTD program soon outgrew the Houston location. Cochran moved the program to Avenger Field in Sweetwater, Texas. Avenger Field was the only all-female military base in the United States. Though still considered civilians, the WFTDs' daily life was like being in the army. They slept in barracks with six women to a room and twelve women to a bathroom. They marched and drilled, exercised together, and were expected to obey orders.

The WFTDs wore oversized men's flight suits, at least until Cochran decided on an official uniform. And like the oversized uniforms, the parachutes female pilots had to work with were too big. Margaret Phelan Taylor was ferrying a plane between Arizona and California

ABBREVIATIONS FOR US FLYING PROGRAMS

ATC	Air Transport Command
USAAF	US Army Air Forces (later changed to USAF)
USAF	US Air Force
WAFS	Women's Auxiliary Ferry Squadron (led by Love)
WASP	Women's Airforce Service Pilots (combined WAFS and WFTD programs)
WFTD	Women's Flying Training Detachment (led by Cochran)

Pilots Lenora Horton, *left*, and Mildred Axton, *right*, show off their oversized flight suits.

when she saw smoke in the cockpit. She'd been taught to bail out, but she knew her parachute was too big. It had been designed to fit a larger man. "They weren't fitted to us. The force of that air and that speed and everything, why that just rips stuff off you. You'd slip right out," said Taylor. She decided to wait. "I thought, 'You know what? I'm not going until I see flame. When I see actual fire, why then I'll jump.'"[17] She landed safely and discovered a burned-out instrument was the problem.

CHAPTER SEVEN
WASPS

The WAFS and the WFTD programs functioned independently at first. In fact, Love and Cochran rarely saw each other. In January 1943, Love began searching for additional airfields to use as air bases for female ferry pilots and for the eventual graduates of Cochran's flying program. It wasn't always easy, in large part because the women needed separate housing from the male pilots.

That summer, Cochran pushed for the two programs to be combined. She wanted a single unit to govern all female fliers. On August 5, the WAFS and WFTD merged into a single unit called the Women Airforce Service Pilots (WASP). General Arnold made

In World War II, the US Army Air Forces relied on 1,074 WASPs to fly military aircraft.

Cochran the head of the entire program, with Love acting as executive of the Ferrying Division.

"All of us realized what a spot we were on. We had to deliver the goods or else. Or else there wouldn't ever be another chance for women pilots in any part of the service."[2]

—Cornelia Fort, WASP

Training and Working

WASP training took place at Avenger Field. Training began before dawn, and pilots spent nearly 12 hours a day at the airfield. Half of the group flew in the morning and attended ground school in the afternoon. The other half did the reverse—ground school in the morning and flying in the afternoon. As pilots trained, the sky was crowded with aircraft, sometimes as many as 40 at a time. They practiced takeoffs and landings, turns, stalls, spins, and night flying. The women received the same training as male pilots except for gunnery practice, because the women were not going to be in combat.

When WASPs graduated, they received a pair of silver wings to put on their uniforms. Then they started ferrying aircraft at one of 120 air bases across the United States.[1]

WASP pilots flew every aircraft operated by the air force. They also flew almost every kind of stateside noncombat mission. They ferried aircraft, towed targets, flew remote-controlled drones, tested aircraft, taught flight classes, and transported cargo and military personnel.

A ferry pilot's life could be unpredictable. Pilots had to be ready to leave at a minute's notice. They had to be flexible enough to fly most anything, anywhere. And they were never sure how long it might take them to reach their destination, because they were dependent upon the weather and any flying assignments that might crop up. A ferry pilot might be gone from base for three days or three weeks; they never knew.

Sometimes ferry pilots flew together in groups to deliver planes, but they had no radios to communicate. Once, when pilot Florene Miller led a group of six planes, she noticed the other planes circling below her. She flew down, got the formation straightened out, then continued on. Again and again, the other planes quit following her and started circling. Finally, Miller, frustrated and irritated,

WASP TRAINING

WASPs received up to 210 hours of flight training in an airplane. They also had up to 560 hours of ground school, including courses such as meteorology and aircraft mechanics.[3] As women with fewer flying hours were admitted to the program, training hours increased.

found an airfield and signaled for everyone to land. To her surprise, she discovered that the pilot who was supposed to be the navigator had lost all of her maps. They had blown out of the open cockpit. By circling, the navigator was trying to signal that someone else should take over.

BY THE NUMBERS

• US female applicants for flight training: 25,000

• Pilots accepted for WFTD/ WASP training: 1,830

• Graduates from WFTD/WASP training: 1,074

• Total number of WASP classes: 18[4]

Attitudes Toward Female Pilots

Attitudes toward women serving as pilots varied, often depending on the attitude of the commanding officer at the base where they served. WASPs who served at the air force bases in Long Beach, California, and Las Vegas, Nevada, felt they were treated the same as men and had plenty of opportunities to fly all different kinds of aircraft, rather than just small trainers. Love transferred to the Long Beach Air Force Base for this very reason.

Oftentimes commanding officers had no idea that female pilots were even coming to their air bases until they stepped out of the aircraft. One WASP remembers her commanding officer saying, "I don't like women in general or women pilots in particular. You are not needed

Jacqueline Cochran, *center*, speaks to a group of WASPs in the ready room at Avenger Field on April 25, 1943.

> "Fear never entered the picture for me. The moment I was in a plane and the instructor turned the controls over to me on the first ride, I knew this was what I wanted to do."[7]
>
> —B. J. Williams, WASP

WASPS AND RACE

Several African-American women applied to the WASP program, and they were all turned down. Cochran felt that she couldn't admit the women as WASPs. It was already an experimental program, and Cochran feared problems with racial discrimination could put the program in jeopardy. Only two women of color served as WASPs: Hazel "Ah Ying" Lee and Maggie Gee. Lee and Gee were Chinese Americans.

here and I will see to it that you don't get into any airplane."[5] Sometimes people thought female pilots were flight attendants or army nurses.

If they flew well, they might be told, "You fly just like a man." Or they might be told, "You did that so well. That was so easy for you. I guess it's not that hard if a woman can do it."[6] On rare occasions, disgruntled people tampered with their planes. Camp Davis in North Carolina seemed to have more problems with this than others. When Cochran investigated one airplane crash at Camp Davis, she discovered someone had put sugar in the gas tank, which caused the engine to quit.

The most typical reaction, though, was simply surprise. Once when Love ferried a P-51 from Long Beach, California, to the East Coast, she asked a military airfield for permission to land. The male radio operator in the control tower said, "Can't see you." Love circled the airfield, waiting for permission to come in. "Ok to come in now?" The radio operator responded, "Where are you? Can't spot you at all."

Tired of waiting, Nancy buzzed the control tower so they couldn't miss her in her P-51. She then asked again if she was cleared to land. The surprised radio operator said, "Cleared to land. I heard a woman's voice and I saw the plane, but I just couldn't figure a woman would be flying a [P-51] Mustang!"[8]

The surprise at women flying wore off as others got used to seeing female pilots and as the women proved their skill as aviators. During World War II, 1,074 WASPs graduated and flew more than 60 million miles (97 million km).[9]

"You and more than 900 of your sisters have shown that you can fly wingtip to wingtip with your brothers. If ever there was a doubt in anyone's mind that women can become skillful pilots, the WASPs have dispelled that doubt."[10]

—General Hap Arnold, in a speech to the last class of WASP graduates

WASP UNIFORMS

When in flight school, the pilots wore mechanic's coveralls, helmets, and flying goggles.

When at ground school, WASPs wore tan pants, a white blouse, and a leather jacket.

When a WASP graduated, she earned a pair of silver wings. She wore these wings on her dress uniform. The silver wings were a great source of pride for WASPs.

When flying in an open cockpit or in cold weather, WASPs wore leather gear.

The official flying uniform was a short blue jacket, a blue shirt, a black tie, pants, and a cap. Pilots also wore the silver wings they earned at graduation on the uniform.

Jacqueline Cochran worked with fashion designers at the New York department store Bergdorf Goodman's to create the official WASP dress uniform. Made out of Santiago blue fabric, the uniform included a belted jacket and straight skirt. WASPs wore this with a white shirt, black tie, beret, and black purse.

CHAPTER EIGHT

AFTER THE WAR

Throughout the war, female pilots had clearly shown they could fly as well as men. However, the circumstances for female pilots began to change as World War II was ending. The WASP program was growing controversial. It had been organized in part to free men for overseas combat. But with the war ending, the War Department said there were enough male pilots to fill current flying needs. Some critics of the WASP program felt the female pilots were taking away jobs from men.

Though they had served their country well, the female pilots of WASP were still considered civilians. This had long-lasting consequences as the pilots began returning home. Cochran and Arnold had originally intended for WASP to become a regular

WASPs take one last look at Avenger Field before returning home when the program ended in 1944.

military program. Most WASPs assumed they would be granted military status eventually. Without this status, WASPs had no military rank, no insurance, and no veterans' benefits.

It looked like the WASP program might be shut down before WASPs got a chance to gain military status. In March 1944, the US Congress debated a law to grant WASP military status. The law was defeated by just 19 votes, in part because male flight instructors fought hard for its defeat.[1]

CLASSIFIED

After the WASP program disbanded in December 1944, its records were sealed and classified until the 1980s. As a result, when historians researched and wrote about World War II, the contributions of WASPs were often left out.

End of an Era

On October 3, 1944, Cochran sent a letter to all WASPs announcing the government would be ending the program. Shutting down the WASP program was expensive, because the US Army Air Forces then had to train male pilots to do the flying jobs WASPs had been doing. This training took four to six months. Planes that needed delivery were left at the factory because WASPs were no longer authorized to fly, and male pilots were not yet ready to take over.

The last group of WASP pilots, class 44-W-10, graduated on December 7, 1944, exactly three years after the bombing of Pearl Harbor. On December 20, the WASP program ended, and 916 female pilots lost their jobs.[2] Their life as military pilots ended abruptly. A few air force bases had closing ceremonies or threw parties, but for many WASPs, they were simply told they had 24 hours to leave.

"Frankly, I didn't know in 1941 whether a slip of a young girl could fight the controls of a B-17 in the heavy weather they would naturally encounter in operational flying. . . . Well, now in 1944, more than two years since WASP first started flying with the Air Forces, we can come to only one conclusion—the entire operation has been a success. It is on the record that women can fly as well as men."[3]

—General Hap Arnold in graduation speech to last WASP class

Soviet Squadrons

In the Soviet Union at the end of the war, the military was gradually released from duty. Before the war, the Soviet government had opposed women serving in the military. During the war, the German invasion created an emergency situation, and women were encouraged to fight. After the war, the Soviet government did not keep any female units. Women were no longer allowed to serve in the military.

Soviet women who had volunteered to fight were expected to return home and focus on their families. In fact, Stalin did not even allow female military personnel to participate in official celebrations that marked the war's end. No official record of their service was created, and their achievements were soon forgotten. Some returned to civil aviation employment, but not many.

Going Home

In the United Kingdom, the ATA program continued until the end of 1945. In 1944, as the war wound down, ferry pools began to close. The all-women ferry pool at Hamble closed in August 1945. Nevertheless, some women kept flying as long as possible.

ATA pilots were released based on seniority, so pilots who had been with the ATA the longest were the last to leave. Rosemary Rees du Cros flew for the ATA even after it officially closed on November 30, 1945. She flew for the White Waltham Ferry Pool until March 1946. Du Cros

Mary Ellis was honored at the seventy-fifth anniversary of the Battle of Britain in August 2015. She ferried approximately 1,000 military aircraft for the ATA.

was grateful she could keep flying, but she said that the White Waltham Ferry Pool was mostly men, and "it felt different to our 'band of sisters' at Hamble."[4]

With the ATA program over, the pilots returned to their homes. Many married and started families, with flying no longer a part of their daily lives. A few, however, were able to turn their piloting skills into peacetime jobs. ATA pilot Joan Hughes went on to become a flight instructor with commercial airlines, and pilot Ann Welch served as the manager for the British Gliding Team for 20 years.

Reflections

The female pilots had mixed feelings about the end of their military flying. Many, particularly the Soviet pilots, were war-weary, and more than ready to go home and get back to normal life. But for many of the pilots, particularly those not in combat, the end of their military flying created a great sense of loss. WASP pilot Teresa James compared her sorrow to the emptiness she felt when her husband died.

Many were tremendously disappointed that, in spite of all their qualifications and experience, there were few flying jobs open to women. The war had opened doors briefly, but after the war, they all seemed to slam shut. Cochran thought

Former WASPs look on as President Obama signs the bill that will award them the Congressional Gold Medal.

approximately 25 percent would be able to find aviation jobs.[7] But Gower made the most accurate prediction when she pointed out that the war had created thousands of male pilots that would want and need jobs. No matter how well-qualified the female pilots were, most of the aviation jobs would go to men.

British ferry pilot Lettice Curtis said the end of the war "did not feel particularly like the happy and glorious day to which we had aspired for the best part of six years."

For female pilots like her who had "nothing to go back to and nowhere particular to go," the end of the war was almost as traumatic as the beginning.[8]

Legacy

In 1949, the US Air Force offered all former WASPs the opportunity to become air force officers. One hundred fifteen women accepted, and 25 accepted full-time officer careers with the air force.[9] Unfortunately, none of these women were ever allowed to fly military aircraft. In the 1960s, the US military once again began letting women serve as jet pilots.

In 1977, WASPs officially became part of the US military. The US

Defense Department announced they would "for the first time" let women fly military planes. Former WASPs were outraged. They were the first women who had flown military planes. WASPs successfully lobbied Congress, and on November 23, 1977, President Jimmy Carter signed into law a bill that recognized the military service of WASPs and granted them veterans' status.

Despite these obstacles, the female pilots of World War II set a standard that continues to inspire people today. During a time when many doubted and criticized them, these bold women persevered, determined to prove their ability. They showed courage and resolve, in spite of setbacks, at a time when their country needed them most.

"The Women Airforce Service Pilots courageously answered their country's call in a time of need while blazing a trail for the brave women who have given and continue to give so much in service to this nation since. Every American should be grateful for their service."[11]

—President Barack Obama, upon awarding the Congressional Gold Medal to WASPs in 2009

TIMELINE

SEPTEMBER 1939

Germany invades Poland; two days later, the United Kingdom and France declare war on Germany. This signals the official beginning of World War II.

1940

Pauline Gower selects eight women to become the first female pilots for the Women's Section of the British ATA; German troops march across Europe, gaining control of Denmark, the Netherlands, Belgium, and France; in July, Germany begins a bombing assault against the United Kingdom; Nancy Love writes to Lieutenant Colonel Robert Olds, providing a list of female pilots who would be qualified to ferry military aircraft.

JUNE 17, 1941

American pilot Jackie Cochran becomes the first woman to ferry a bomber across the Atlantic Ocean.

JUNE 22, 1941

The war intensifies as Germany invades the Soviet Union in Operation Barbarossa.

OCTOBER 8, 1941

Marina Raskova receives permission to organize female combat pilots for the Soviet Union.

DECEMBER 1941

Germany's ally Japan attacks the US ships stationed at Pearl Harbor, Hawaii; the next day, the United States declares war on Japan; on December 11, the United States declares war on Germany.

SEPTEMBER 10, 1942

US Secretary of War Henry Stimson announces the formation of WAFS under the leadership of Nancy Love.

SEPTEMBER 15, 1942

Stimson announces a second group of women pilots, WFTDs, under the leadership of Jackie Cochran.

SEPTEMBER 21, 1942
The first WAFS pilots are sworn in at New Castle Army Air Base in Wilmington, Delaware.

NOVEMBER 1942
The first class of WFTDs arrive at Howard Hughes Field in Houston, Texas, for training.

FEBRUARY 18, 1943
The second test flight of the B-29 Superfortress ends in a crash, and many male pilots refuse to fly it.

AUGUST 5, 1943
The WAFS and WFTD programs merge to form the Women Airforce Service Pilots (WASP).

MAY 1944
Paul Tibbets trains WASPs Dora Dougherty and Didi Johnson to fly the B-29. A few weeks later they begin giving demonstration flights to prove the B-29's safety.

DECEMBER 20, 1944
The WASP program officially ends.

NOVEMBER 30, 1945
The British ATA program officially ends.

NOVEMBER 23, 1977
President Jimmy Carter signs a bill into law that gives WASPs veteran status.

1993
Women are cleared to fly combat missions for the US Air Force.

1995
Martha McSally becomes the first US female pilot to fly in combat.

2009
President Barack Obama Awards the Congressional Gold Medal to WASPS.

ESSENTIAL FACTS

- Nancy Love organized the Women's Auxiliary Ferrying Squadron (WAFS) in 1942. WAFS later became part of the WASP program.

- Jacqueline Cochran organized the Women's Flying Training Detachment (WFTD) in 1942. The WFTD later became part of the WASP program.

- Pauline Gower championed women flying in the United Kingdom's Air Auxiliary Transport (ATA). Gower led the female pilots of the ATA beginning in 1939.

- Marina Raskova was a Soviet pilot who used her connections with Soviet leader Joseph Stalin to create three regiments of female combat pilots.

KEY STATISTICS

- Twenty-five thousand women applied to be in the WFTD/WASP program. Of those applicants, 1,830 were accepted and 1,074 graduated.

- Thirty-eight WASPs died while serving their country.

- From 1942 to 1944, WASPs flew more than 60 million miles (97 million km).

- WAFS and the WFTD merged on August 5, 1943, and became the WASP program.

- WASPs served at 120 air bases within the United States.

IMPACT ON HISTORY

It is hard to overstate the impact WASPs had on history. They served their country as the first group of women to fly military aircraft. They ferried planes, tested new aircraft, instructed other pilots, and freed male pilots for combat duty. They also proved that women could pilot massive bombers, nimble fighters, and everything in between. The work of the WASPs changed the role of women in the military, and they were no longer viewed only as nurses or secretaries. The bravery and determination of WASPs opened the way for today's female combat pilots.

QUOTE

"Women are not born with wings, neither are men for that matter. Wings are won by hard work, just as proficiency is won in any profession."

—Pauline Gower

GLOSSARY

AUXILIARY
Reserves separate from the regular armed forces and used for assistance during wartime.

AVIATOR
A pilot.

BARNSTORMER
A pilot who traveled across the country performing stunts in the air.

BARRACK
A building used as housing for member of the military.

CIVILIAN
A person not serving in the armed forces.

DETACHMENT
A group of troops selected for a special mission.

DOGFIGHT
An aerial battle between single opposing planes or groups of planes.

FERRY
To transport an aircraft a relatively short distance by flying it from one place to another.

FLIGHT ENGINEER
A crew member who is responsible for an aircraft's engines.

GLIDER
An aircraft that does not have an engine.

HYDRAULIC CONTROL
Control powered by liquid pressure rather than manual power.

INFRASTRUCTURE
The physical structures, such as roads, railways, and power plants, that make it possible for a city or nation to function.

NAVIGATOR
A crew member who plans a route from one location to the next.

PRESSURIZED CABIN
The airtight body of an aircraft that has oxygen pumped into it, allowing pilots to safely fly aircraft at high altitudes.

REGIMENT
A military unit that is made up of several large groups.

SOLO
To fly a plane as the only person onboard.

SQUADRON
A group of aircraft making up a single unit within an air force.

TRAINER
An airplane used for training pilots.

ADDITIONAL
RESOURCES

SELECTED BIBLIOGRAPHY

Merry, Lois K. *Women Military Pilots of World War II*. Jefferson, NC: McFarland, 2011. Print.

Strebe, Amy Goodpaster. *Flying for Her Country*. Washington, DC: Potomac, 2009. Print.

Verges, Marianne. *On Silver Wings*. New York: Random, 1991. Print.

FURTHER READINGS

Adams, Simon. *DK Eyewitness Books: World War II*. London: Dorling Kindersley, 2007. Print.

Gibson, Karen Bush. *Women Aviators*. Chicago, IL: Chicago Review Press, 2013. Print.

Winchester, Jim, ed. *Aircraft of World War II*. London: Chartwell, 2012. Print.

WEBSITES

To learn more about Hidden Heroes, visit **booklinks.abdopublishing.com**. These links are routinely monitored and updated to provide the most current information available.

For more information on this subject, contact or visit the following organizations:

THE NATIONAL MUSEUM OF THE US AIR FORCE
1100 Spaatz Street
Wright-Patterson Air Force Base, OH 45433
937-253-4629
http://www.nationalmuseum.af.mil/Visit/MuseumExhibits/
WWIIGallery.aspx
The National Museum of the US Air Force has a World War II Gallery, which houses one of the world's top collections of WWII aircraft. Also available is the exhibit *WASP: Breaking Ground for Today's Female USAF Pilots*. The museum is located at historic Wright Field, at Wright-Patterson Air Force Base, near Dayton, Ohio.

THE NATIONAL WASP WWII MUSEUM
210 Avenger Field Road
Sweetwater, TX 79556
325-235-0099
http://waspmuseum.org/
The National WASP WWII Museum tells the story of the first women to fly US military aircraft. The museum is located in Sweetwater, Texas, home of Avenger Field, where the WASPs trained.

SOURCE NOTES

CHAPTER 1. "TRAIN TWO WOMEN TO FLY IT."

1. Earl Swinhart. "B-29." *Aviation History Online Museum*. Aviation History Online Museum, 3 Aug. 2000. Web. 1 May 2016.

2. Martha Lockwood. "Women's Legacy Parallels Air Force History." *Air Force News Service*. US Air Force, 18 Sept. 2014. Web. 9 Sept. 2016.

3. Amy Nathan. *Yankee Doodle Gals*. Washington, DC: National Geographic, 2013. Print. 73.

4. "Heavy Bomber Development." *USAF*. USAF, 1951. Web. 15 May 2016.

5. "Paul Tibbets Interview." *WASP Archive*. TWU, 24 Feb 1997. Web. 5 May 2016.

6. Negar Tekeei. "Fly Girl." *Northwestern*. NU, Spring 2002. Web. 28 May 2016.

7. Amy Nathan. *Yankee Doodle Gals*. Washington, DC: Nat Geo, 2013. Print. 73.

8. "Paul Tibbets Interview." *WASP Archive*. TWU, 24 Feb 1997. Web. 5 May 2016.

9. "Fly Girls." *American Experience*. WGBH, 1999. Web. 9 Sept. 2016.

10. Ibid.

11. Harry McKeown. "Letter to Dora Dougherty Strother." *The Woman's Collection*. TWU, 2 Aug. 1995. Web. 30 June 2016.

12. "Fly Girls." *American Experience*. WGBH, 1999. Web. 9 Sept. 2016.

13. "Facts." *WASP on the Web*. Wings Across America, n.d. Web. 9 Sept. 2016.

14. Negar Tekeei. "Fly Girl." *Northwestern*. NU, Spring 2002. Web. 28 May 2016.

CHAPTER 2. PIONEERS

1. "Balloon Flight." *Britannica Library*. Encyclopædia, 2016. Web. 5 July 2016.

2. Tracy Irons-Georges. "History of Human Flight." *Encyclopedia of Flight*. Pasadena, CA: Salem, 2002. eBook. 344.

3. Alison McLean. "Mar. Anniversaries." *Smithsonian Magazine*. Smithsonian, Mar. 2010. Web. 10 Aug. 2016.

4. Tom Longden. "Neta Snook." *Des Moines Register*. Des Moines Register, n.d. Web. 25 Aug. 2016.

5. Bruce Gould. "Milady Takes the Air." *North American Review*. North American Review, Dec. 1929. Web. 29 July 2016.

6. Ibid.

7. "1929 Air Race." *99 News Magazine*. Ninety Nines, 1999. Web. 12 Aug. 2016.

8. Ibid.

9. Ibid.

10. "Amelia Earhart." *American Experience*. WGBH, 1993. Web. 9 Sept. 2016.

11. Karen Bush Gibson. *Women Aviators*. Chicago, IL: Review, 2013. Print. 46–48.

12. Ibid.

13. Ibid.

14. "Amelia Earhart." *Britannica Library*. Britannica, 2016. Web. 6 July 2016.

15. "The Ninety-Nines from 1929 to 1959." *Ninety-Nines*. The Ninety-Nines, Inc., n.d. Web. 28 Oct. 2016.

16. Louise Thaden. *High, Wide, and Frightened*. U of Arkansas, 2004. Print. 151.

CHAPTER 3. WAR IN THE SKIES

1. "The Rise of the Luftwaffe." *RAF Museum*. RAF, n.d. Web. 12 July 2016.

2. Hanna Reitsch. *Flying Is My Life.* Trans. Lawrence Wilson. New York: Putnam, 1954. Print. 3.

3. Negar Tekeei. "Fly Girl." *Northwestern.* NU, Spring 2002. Web. 28 May 2016.

4. Theresa L Kraus. "The CAA Helps America Prepare for World War II." *Federal Aviation Administration.* FAA, n.d. Web. 28 July 2016.

5. Sally Van Wagenen Keil. *Those Wonderful Women in Their Flying Machines.* New York: Four Directions, 1979. Print. 70.

6. Amy Nathan. *Yankee Doodle Gals.* Washington, DC: Nat Geo, 2013. Print. 8.

7. Cornelia Fort. "At the Twilight's Last Gleaming." *Women's Home Companion.* Wings Across America, July 1943. Web. 2 June 2016.

8. Ibid.

9. Earl F. Ziemke. "World War II: Early Campaigns." *Encyclopedia Americana.* Grolier, 2016. Web. 8 July 2016.

10. John W. Carpenter. "Battle of Britain." *Encyclopedia Americana.* Grolier, 2016. Web. 8 July 2016.

11. "Battle of Britain." *Britannica Library.* Britannica, Web. 18 June 2015.

12. Cornelia Fort. "At the Twilight's Last Gleaming." *Women's Home Companion.* Wings Across America, July 1943. Web. 2 June 2016.

13. Ibid.

14. "Procurement at Flood Time." *The Army Air Forces in World War II.* HyperWar, n.d. Web. 9 Sept. 2016.

CHAPTER 4. "ATA-GIRLS"

1. Yona Zeldis McDonough. "The Women's RAF." *Air & Space Magazine.* Smithsonian, May 2012. Web. 1 June 2016.

2. "The Forgotten Pilots." *BBC.* BBC, 2005. Web. 5 June 2016.

3. "Pauline Gower." *RAF Museum.* RAF Museum, n.d. Web. 6 July 2016.

4. Lois K. Merry. *Women Military Pilots of World War II.* Jefferson, NC: McFarland, 2011. Print. 36.

5. Emily Urquhart. "This, for Me, Was Freedom." *Globe and Mail,* 30 Oct. 2004. Web. 4 June 2016.

6. Ibid.

7. "Anything to Anywhere." *Air Transport Auxiliary Museum.* Maidenhead Heritage Centre, n.d. Web. 3 June 2016.

8. Rosemary du Cros. *ATA Girl: Memoirs of a Wartime Ferry Pilot.* London: Frederick Muller, 1983. Print. 84.

9. "Home." *The Ferry Pilots of the ATA.* The ATA, 2016. Web. 9 Sept. 2016.

10. Tessa Stone. "Women's Section of the Air Transport Auxiliary." *Oxford Dictionary of National Biography.* Oxford: Oxford UP, 2004. Web. 4 June 2016.

CHAPTER 5. SOVIET PILOTS

1. Tracy Irons-Georges. "History of Human Flight." *Encyclopedia of Flight.* Pasadena, CA: Salem, 2002. eBook. 772.

2. "History of Airpower." *International Military and Defense Encyclopedia.* International Military and Defense Encyclopedia, n.d. Web. 14 June 2016.

3. Ibid.

SOURCE NOTES
CONTINUED

4. Ibid.

5. Lois K. Merry. *Women Military Pilots of World War II*. Jefferson, NC: McFarland, 2011. Print. 14–16.

6. Ibid.

7. Ibid.

8. Amy Goodpaster Strebe. *Flying for Her Country*. Washington, DC: Potomac, 2009. Print. 20.

9. Ibid.

10. Ibid.

11. Bruce Lambert. "Valentina S. Grizodubova." *New York Times*. New York Times, 1 May 1993. Web. 25 Aug. 2016.

12. Anne Noggle. *A Dance with Death*. College Station, TX: Texas A&M, 1994. Print. 157.

13. Ibid.

14. Megan Garber. "Night Witches" *Atlantic*. Atlantic, 15 July 2013. Web. 1 May 2016.

15. Ibid.

16. Amy Goodpaster Strebe. *Flying for Her Country*. Washington, DC: Potomac, 2009. Print. 26.

17. Anne Noggle. *A Dance with Death*. College Station, TX: Texas A&M, 1994. Print. 31–34.

18. Lois K. Merry. *Women Military Pilots of World War II*. Jefferson, NC: McFarland, 2011. Print. 112.

19. Amy Goodpaster Strebe. *Flying for Her Country*. Washington, DC: Potomac, 2009. Print. 19.

20. Henry Sakaida. *Heroines of the Soviet Union 1941–45*. Osceola, WI: Osprey, 2003. Print. 18.

CHAPTER 6. WAFS & WFTD

1. James W. Williams. *A History of Army Aviation*. Lincoln, NE: US Army Aviation Museum Foundation, 2005. Print. 28.

2. Mark Betancourt. "World War II: The Movie." *Air & Space Magazine*. Smithsonian, Mar. 2012. Web. 1 July 2016.

3. Marianne Verges. *On Silver Wings*. New York: Random, 1991. Print. 17.

4. "History of the WASP." *WASP Archive*. TWU Libraries, n.d. Web. 31 May 2016.

5. Sarah Byrn Rockman. *Nancy Love and the WASP Ferry Pilots of World War II*. Denton, TX: U of North Texas, 2008. Print. 21.

6. Marianne Verges. *On Silver Wings*. New York: Random, 1991. Print. 10.

7. "By the Numbers." *WWII Museum*. WWII Museum, n.d. Web. 11 Aug. 2016.

8. Marianne Verges. *On Silver Wings*. New York: Random, 1991. Print. 11.

9. Ibid.

10. Ibid.

11. Ibid.

12. "My Day, Sept. 1, 1942," *E. Roosevelt Papers*. GWU, n.d. Web. 10 Aug. 2016.

13. Marianne Verges. *On Silver Wings*. New York: Random, 1991. Print. 43.

14. "WASP Training." *WASP Archive*. TWU Libraries, n.d. Web. 31 May 2016.

15. Marianne Verges. *On Silver Wings*. New York: Random, 1991. Print. 43.

16. "WASP Training." *WASP Archive*. TWU Libraries, n.d. Web. 31 May 2016.

17. Susan Stamberg. "Female WWII Pilots: The Original Fly Girls." *NPR News*. NPR, 9 Mar. 2010. Web. 9 Sept. 2016.

CHAPTER 7. WASPS

1. "History of the WASP." *WASP Archive*. TWU Libraries, n.d. Web. 31 May 2016.

2. Cornelia Fort. "At the Twilight's Last Gleaming." *Women's Home Companion*. Wings Across America, July 1943. Web. 2 June 2016.

3. "History of the WASP." *WASP Archive*. TWU Libraries, n.d. Web. 31 May 2016.

4. Jacqueline Cochran. "Final Report on Women Pilot Program." *Army Air Forces Report 6-1262, 1945*. Eisenhower Library, n.d. Web. 25 Aug. 2016.

5. Lois K. Merry. *Women Military Pilots of World War II*. Jefferson, NC: McFarland, 2011. Print. 50.

6. Ibid.

7. Amy Nathan. *Yankee Doodle Gals*. Washington, DC: National Geographic, 2013. Print. 15.

8. Marianne Verges. *On Silver Wings*. New York: Random, 1991. Print. 178–179.

9. Jacqueline Cochran. "Final Report on Women Pilot Program." *Army Air Forces Report 6-1262, 1945*. Eisenhower Library, n.d. Web. 25 Aug. 2016.

10. General "Hap" Arnold. "Address before WASP Ceremony." *WASP Graduation*. Wings Across America, n.d. Web. 9 Sept. 2016.

CHAPTER 8. AFTER THE WAR

1. "WASP Militarization." *WASP Archive*. TWU Libraries, n.d. Web. 31 May 2016.

2. Ibid.

3. General "Hap" Arnold. "Address before WASP Ceremony." *WASP Graduation*. Wings Across America, n.d. Web. 9 Sept. 2016.

4. Rosemary du Cros. *ATA Girl: Memoirs of a Wartime Ferry Pilot*. London: Frederick Muller, 1983. Print. 86.

5. Rowan Scarborough. "She Has the Right Stuff." *Washington Times*. Washington Times, n.d. Web. 25 Mar. 2013.

6. Ibid.

7. Lois K. Merry. *Women Military Pilots of World War II*. Jefferson, NC: McFarland, 2011. Print. 114–115.

8. Ibid. 124.

9. Anne Noggle. *For God, Country, and the Thrill of It*. College Station, TX: Texas A&M UP, 1990. Print. 14.

10. Huma Khan. "First Female Airforce Pilots Get Gold Honor." *ABC News*. ABC, n.d. Web. 10 Mar. 2010.

11. "Congressional Gold Medal to Women Airforce Service Pilots." *White House*. White House, 1 July 2009. Web. 9 Sept. 2016.

INDEX

ABOUT THE
AUTHOR

A freelance writer who writes for both adults and children, Shannon Baker Moore has written four other books for Abdo Publishing: *The Korean War, King Tut's Tomb, A History of Music*, and *Harlem Hellfighters.* Shannon and her family have lived throughout the United States and currently call Saint Louis, Missouri, home. There, Shannon volunteers as Assistant Regional Advisor for the Missouri chapter of SCBWI (Society of Children's Book Writers & Illustrators).